Babes Remember

Babes Remember

UNFORGETTABLE PEOPLE, PLACES, AND THINGS FROM THE '50S AND '60S

Jill Larson Sundberg
with Michael Larson

CONARI PRESS

First published in 2005 by Conari Press, an imprint of Red Wheel/Weiser, LLC
York Beach, ME
With offices at:
368 Congress Street
Boston, MA 02210
www.redwheelweiser.com

Library of Congress Cataloging-in-Publication Data
Sundberg, Jill Larson.
   Babes remember : unforgettable people, places, and things from the 50s and
60s / Jill Larson Sundberg with Michael Larson.
      p. cm.
   ISBN 1-57324-251-9
   1. Popular culture—United States—History—20th century—Miscellanea. 2.
United States—Civilization—1945—-Miscellanea. 3. United States—Social
life and customs—1945-1970—Miscellanea. I. Larson, Michael. II. Title.
   E169.12.S869 2005
   306'.0973'09045—dc22

                              2005004686

Typeset in FrankfurterMedium, Bodoni Book, Onyx, and PumpEF-medium
by Jill Feron/FeronDesign
Printed in Canada; Friesens

12 11 10 09 08 07 06 05
  8 7 6 5 4 3 2 1

The paper used in this publication meets the minimum requirements of the American National Standard for Information Sciences—Permanence of Paper for Printed Library Materials Z39.48-1992 (R1997).

I would like to dedicate this book to those who attended the Watonwan County District 32 Country School, Long Lake Lutheran Church, and the St. James High School (St. James, Minnesota) Class of 1964 for sharing all of these wonderful memories with me!

Contents

Introduction

My friend Barb Hendricks and I were just relaxing and chatting one day and I asked her if she remembered pixie haircuts. That question led to another and began one of the most enjoyable conversations I've ever had. We reminisced about poodle skirts, spit curls, autograph dogs, slumber parties, Buffalo Bob, Froggy, Dick Tracy, and so on.

We asked each other, "Do you remember . . .?" about things such as the name of Roy Rogers' horse, the name of the Lone Ranger's sidekick, panda sweaters, bucket purses, and trying to sleep on brush rollers. We ended up howling!

So I decided a book such as this just might spur some fun conversations about "days gone by" for other people. You can also use this book as a reference when telling your grandchildren and/or the younger generation about *your* childhood. Each page is a conversation piece. Enjoy!

—JILL LARSON SUNDBERG

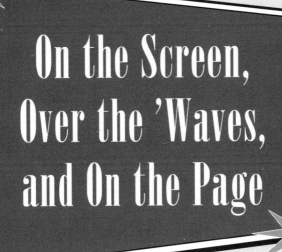

On the Screen,
Over the 'Waves,
and On the Page

The $64,000 Question

One of the most memorable contestants on this popular 1950s quiz show was Teddy Nadler. A government clerk from St. Louis who worked for $1.78 an hour, Nadler won a total of $264,000 on *The $64,000 Question* and *The $64,000 Challenge* in 1957. What made Nadler particularly intriguing was the quiz show topic he chose: "Everything."

77 Sunset Strip

Abbott and Costello

The Andy Griffith Show

In its eight years on the air from 1960 to 1968, *The Andy Griffith Show* never dropped below seventh place in the

Nielsen rankings, and it was Number 1 the year it ceased production.

Andy Griffith played Sheriff Andy Taylor, the fair-minded, easygoing sheriff in Mayberry, N.C. Andy, a widower, applied his old-fashioned common sense to raising his son Opie (Ronny Howard), a task he shared with his Aunt Bee (Frances Bavier).

The townspeople—and the cast of actors who portrayed them—were crucial to the success of the show. Gomer Pyle (Jim Nabors) and his cousin Goober (George Lindsey) came out of the "bumpkin" tradition that had been developed in films, popular literature, and comic strips. Town barber Floyd Lawson

(Howard McNear) was a font of misinformation and the forerunner of *Cheers'* Cliff Clavin.

Much of Andy's time was spent controlling his earnest but overzealous deputy, Barney Fife (Don Knotts). Don played the comic and pathetic sides of the character with equal aplomb. He won four Emmy Awards for his work.

Andy's Gang

As the World Turns

Axel and His Dog

For young television viewers in the Upper Midwest, it was Clellan Card as "Axel" who stole our hearts. We would race home to our farm in the late afternoon to watch *Axel and His Dog*. Axel wore granny glasses, sported a comical moustache, and spoke with a strong

Scandinavian accent that created such words as "Minnesnapolis" and "Minnesnowta." The show featured the Little Rascals and their antics as well as a dog, Towser, and a cat, Tallulah. We never saw Towser. We only saw his gigantic paw holding onto Axel, usually resting on Axel's shoulder and teasing Axel's face when he barked. At the end of the show, Axel would recite one of the more famous sign-offs in Minnesota television history:

> *Birdie with a yellow bill,*
> *Hopped upon my window sill,*
> *Cocked his shining eye and said,*
> *"What did you get for your birthday,*
> *Smarty . . . Pants?"*

Clellan Card's death in 1966 was mourned by fans young and old.

Benny Kubelsky

Benny Kubelsky left Waukegan, Illinois, and found fame in Hollywood as a star of stage, screen, and television. Oh, yes, and a star of radio, too. Along the way he changed his name to Jack Benny.

Bobby Benson and the B-Bar-B

The Bowery Boys

Camelot

Captain Kangaroo

Kids loved *Captain Kangaroo*. Bob Keeshan played the Captain. Do you remember who played Mister Greenjeans?

The Carol Burnett Show

This show produced some of the greatest humor of the era. Filled with comedy sketches and spoofs of TV series and movies, it was variety at its best. Among the comic characterizations were Mr. Tudball and Mrs. Wiggins. In these skits, Carol Burnett played an inept office worker with a frustrated boss (Tim Conway). In the Ed and Eunice sketches, Carol and Harvey Korman played a married couple constantly at odds with Eunice's mother (Vicki Lawrence). Tim Conway starred as the young hard-of-hearing friend who worked in Korman's hardware store. The sketch was the basis for the TV series *Mama's Family* starring Vicki Lawrence.

Of all the parodies performed on the show, a spoof of the film *Gone with the Wind* is one of the best remembered. Burnett played Starlett O'Hara, who tried to tempt the debonair Rat Butler (Harvey Korman) by using drapes and a curtain rod to make an elegant gown.

Champion

Gene Autry's "Wonder Horse of the West."

Charles Van Doren

The Cisco Kid

Based loosely upon the well-known O. Henry short story, *The Cisco Kid* became a great TV Western series starring

Duncan Renaldo as Cisco riding Diablo and Leo Carrillo as Poncho riding Loco.

Cracked magazine

Poor cousin to *Mad* magazine

Davy Crockett

"King of the Wild Frontier"

Dick and Jane

"See Spot run."

Dick Van Dyke

The Dinah Shore Chevy Show

Doctor Kildare

The Donna Reed Show

Dragnet • • • • • • • • • • • •

East Side Kids

Edd "Kookie" Brynes

Edward R. Murrow

Father Knows Best

Fearless Fosdick

Froggy

"Plunk your magic twanger, Froggy."

Gabby Hayes

Gene Autry

There were always two cowboys for us—Gene Autry and Roy Rogers. We sometimes got their sidekicks mixed up: Gene Autry had Pat Butrum and Roy Rogers had Pat Brady. We knew Gene Autry as the Singing Cowboy from the Melody Ranch.

Gilligan's Island

Gunsmoke

We watched *Gunsmoke* as a family on Saturday nights on a black-and-white TV.

The Honeymooners

Considered one of the greatest television shows ever, *The Honeymooners* was originally created by Jackie Gleason as a sketch for the *Cavalcade of Stars*, a popular variety show that Gleason hosted regularly in the early 1950s. Though the first Honeymooners sketch lasted less than five minutes, the down-to-earth situations and characters appealed to the American people, who understood and empathized with the big-mouthed bus driver Ralph Kramden, his practical wife Alice, and their friends and neighbors, the Nortons. Gleason left the *Cavalcade of Stars* in 1952 and moved with *The Honeymooners* to his own program, *The Jackie Gleason Show*, on CBS. Art Carney and Joyce Randolph, who played Ed and Trixie Norton, moved with Gleason. Pert Kelton, the original Alice, did not and was replaced by New York actress Audrey Meadows.

And awaaayyyyyy we go!

The Howdy Doody Show

One of the first and most popular children's TV programs in the 1950s, *The Howdy Doody Show* premiered in March of 1948. Howdy was an all-American boy marionette with red hair, forty-eight freckles (one for each state in the Union), and a permanent smile.

Among the many unusual marionettes in Doodyville was Phineas T. Bluster, Doodyville's mayor. Bluster's eyebrows went straight up when he was surprised. His naïve young assistant, Dilly Dally, wiggled his ears when he was frustrated. Flub-a-Dub was a whimsical character who was a combination of eight animals.

Bob Smith, born in Buffalo, New York, became Buffalo Bob when he joined the cast as the great white leader of the Sigafoose tribe. One of the few female characters on the show was Princess Summerfall Winterspring of the Tinka Tonka tribe, who started out as a puppet and was later

transformed into a real live princess, played by Judy Tyler. Much of the mayhem was created by an endearing, mischievous clown named Clarabell Hornblow, played by Bob Keeshan, who later became Captain Kangaroo.

Humphrey Bogart

Huntz Hall

I love Lucy

Lucy, Ricky, Fred,
and Ethel were a part of
everyone's family.

Jack LaLanne

TV's first fitness guru, LaLanne hosted an exercise show for thirty-four years. Starting in 1951, he directed America's housewives in the proper form for sit-ups and push-ups to the accompaniment of organ music.

LaLanne sometimes did outrageous stunts to show off his physical prowess. In 1956, for example, the then forty-two-year-old performed 1,033 push-ups in twenty-three minutes on the TV show *You Asked for It.* At age seventy, he towed boats while swimming across Long Beach Harbor handcuffed.

Dismissing old age as a myth, LaLanne says older folks should get out of their easy chairs and "work at living." At age eighty-nine, he still hits the gym every day at 5:00 AM to lift weights and swim for two hours.

Jack Paar

Jack Webb

James Dean

Johnny Weissmuller

Of the forty-eight *Tarzan* movies, the Romanian/ Austrian-born muscular Olympic swimmer Johnny Weissmuller appeared in an even dozen. It is Weissmuller who is still most closely associated with the Tarzan character, just as Maureen O'Sullivan (1911–1998) will forever be identified as Tarzan's mate, Jane. Few, if any, of the many later *Tarzan* films can match the character and charm of the Weissmuller-O'Sullivan films. Following the Tarzan series,

Weissmuller made sixteen Jungle Jim movies (basically Tarzan with clothes on) for Columbia.

Judy Garland

Lassie

We watched *Lassie* on Sunday nights, and I ate Campbell's vegetable beef soup while watching it because Campbell's sponsored the show and the commercial always made me hungry for soup.

Laurel and Hardy

Lawrence Welk

Leo Gorcey

Life magazine

The Life of Riley

The Little Rascals

Spanky, Alfalfa, Darla, Stymie, Porky, Buckwheat, Butch, Woym, Waldo, and Petey

The Lone Ranger and Tonto

Clayton Moore played the Lone Ranger, who rode the great white horse called Silver, and Jay Silverheels played Tonto, who rode a paint called Scout. Clayton Moore premiered as the Lone Ranger in 1949. Silverheels was a full-blooded Mohawk Indian from the Six Nations Indian Reservation in Ontario, Canada. He played in the entire *Lone Ranger* TV series as well as the two feature-length

motion pictures *The Lone Ranger* and *The Lone Ranger and the Lost City of Gold.*

Fred Foy became the most famous announcer for *The Lone Ranger.* Selected in 1948, his stentorian delivery of, "Return with us now to those thrilling days of yesteryear . . ." delighted his audience for years and helped the program achieve even greater popularity and status as an outstanding example of radio's Golden Age.

Look magazine

Mad magazine

What, me worry?

The Marx Brothers

Mission Impossible

The Mod Squad

The Mouseketeers

There were thirty-nine Mouseketeers and two adult hosts during the original *Mickey Mouse Club*'s four-year run from 1955 to 1959. Jimmie Dodd served as the adult leader of the Mouseketeers, and he wrote many of the songs used in the show, including "The Mickey Mouse Club March." Dodd continued to work for the Disney organization until his death from a heart attack in 1964.

Annette Funicello was the most famous Mouseketeer. In 1987, she was diagnosed with multiple sclerosis. Since then, she has been involved in business ventures with a line of collectable teddy bears and her own perfume, *Cello*. The proceeds go to neurological research.

M-i-c-k-e-y

M-o-u-s-e!!

Myron Floren

Myron Floren achieved most of his fame with the Lawrence Welk Orchestra. It started the night Floren and his wife went dancing at the Casa Loma ballroom in St. Louis where Welk was appearing. Welk invited Floren up on stage to play a number. Floren chose "Lady of Spain." The crowd went wild, and Welk offered Floren a job that very night. In 1950, Floren joined the band and stayed until the show's end in 1982, directing the band whenever Welk was away. Today, Floren continues to play his accordion throughout the United States.

Nellybelle

Pat Brady, Roy Rogers' sidekick, drove a stubborn Jeep called Nellybelle.

The Outlaw

Ozzie and Harriet

The Adventures of Ozzie and Harriet began in the fall of 1952. The show ran fourteen seasons with 435 episodes. Eventually, sons David and Ricky would join their parents on the show, which had its start on the radio.

Pat Boone

Patti Page

Peter Pan

The Pinky Lee Show

Red Skelton

Ricky Nelson

Named Eric Hilliard Nelson by his entertainer parents, Ozzie and Harriet Nelson, Ricky Nelson was born on May 8, 1940, in Teaneck, New Jersey. Eventually, Ricky and his older brother David joined their parents on *The Adventures of Ozzie and Harriet* TV show. Seen weekly in the living rooms of America, the Nelson boys were the object of much affection from young girls. When Ricky was sixteen, he made a record and performed Fats Domino's "I'm Walkin'" on the *Ozzie and Harriet* show. He went on to star in TV sitcoms and pioneered many forms of music

including rockabilly, rock 'n' roll, country rock, and the California Sound.

Rocky and His Friends

Rod Serling

Roy Rogers & Dale Evans

The man who became Roy Rogers, the King of the Cowboys, grew up as Leonard Sly. We knew Dale Evans as the Queen of the West.

Satchmo

The Saturday Evening Post

Sergeant Preston of the Yukon

"On King, on you huskies."

Shane

Silent Spring

Sky King

'Splain

Desi Arnaz as Ricky Ricardo:
"I'll 'splain."

Lucille Ball as Lucy:
"Okay, 'splain."

Tropic of Cancer

Twiggy

The Twilight Zone

Uncle Miltie

The Virginian

Wagon Train

Who's on First?

Wild Bill Hickock and Jingles

Winky Dink and You

The Wizard of Oz

Zorro

Rockin' and Reelin'

33 1/3s and 45s

Alvin and the Chipmunks

At the Hop

This was my first rock 'n' roll record—a "45."

The Beach Boys

The Beatles

We will always remember The Beatles as The Fab Four: John Winston Lennon, James Paul McCartney, George Harrison, and Richard "Ringo Starr" Starkey. "Love Me Do" was the Beatles' first single and hit. The song that really caught people's attention, however, was "I Want to Hold Your Hand," performed on the Ed Sullivan show on February 9, 1964. This was The Beatles' first live appearance in the United States, and the event still holds the

record for largest viewing audience. It also marked the start of the phenomenon we came to call "Beatlemania."

The Beatles are the only band to ever hold the top five positions on America's singles' chart at the same time. They also have the most Number 1 songs (twenty) and albums (sixteen) and have sold more than seventy million albums in the United States alone.

The Big Bopper

Bill Haley and the Comets

"Rock Around the Clock"

Blue Moon

Buddy Holly

Chubby Checker

It took nearly fourteen months, from June 1959 to August 1960, for Chubby Checker's version of "The Twist" to catch on. Checker worked hard at promoting the record, undertaking a nonstop round of interviews, TV appearances, and live performances. After three months of demonstrating the Twist dance moves, he had lost nearly thirty pounds.

The Twist became a dance sensation and scores of twist tunes followed "The Peppermint Twist," "The Oliver Twist," and dozens of variations. This opened up a floodgate of new dances including the Fly, the Hully Gully, the Popeye, the Jerk, the Boogaloo, the Philly, the Locomotion, the Swim, the Hucklebuck, and the Funky Broadway. Many of these were introduced by Checker, who also kicked off the next really big dance craze: the Pony.

Dick Clark and American Bandstand

The show that ultimately became *American Bandstand* originally aired in 1952 on WFIL-TV in Philadelphia and was called Bob Horn's Bandstand after its host, Bob Horn. Dick Clark took over as host in July of 1956 and the show acquired its new name. For the better part of four decades, Dick Clark became incredibly influential in determining teenage pop music tastes in the United States. It helped that next door to the Philadelphia studio was a large high school whose students were only too ready to be part of the live audience.

Almost all of America's new teen performers (and a few older ones) clamored to lip-synch their hits on the show, and Clark could create new dance fads overnight. Clark avoided the payola scandals of the '50s and '60s to become one of the most powerful business people in the United States.

Elvis Presley

Elvis Presley was an idol to many of us during the '50s and '60s (and, indeed, still is). Elvis stood out, and . . . he shook us up! With sleepy eyes, sideburns, expressive lips, and a deep, smooth voice, he left many teen girls swooning.

One of the biggest events of 1956 was Elvis's appearance on the Ed Sullivan show. When he appeared on September 9, we wanted to watch him move as much as hear him sing. But Ed Sullivan refused to let the cameras drift below Presley's waist. We were disappointed that we didn't get to see all his cool "Elvis the Pelvis" moves, but his performance was exciting anyway.

The Everly Brothers

The first song Don and Phil Everly recorded was "Bye Bye Love," written by Felice and Boudleaux Bryant, a husband-and-wife songwriting team who had an ability to capture the imagination of the average teen.

The song was rejected by thirty other acts before the Everlys and their musical mentor, Chet Atkins, took it on and added something to it. They kept the high, keening harmonies, but backed them with robust acoustic guitars and a rock-'n'-roll beat that owed something to Bo Diddley. At the time, country music was in a bit of decline as rock-'n'-roll music, led by Elvis Presley, Chuck Berry, Little Richard and others, was becoming increasingly popular. The Everly Brothers' recording of "Bye Bye Love" rejuvenated the music business in Nashville and established Don and Phil Everly as legendary performers.

How Much Is That Doggie in the Window?

My cousin Lowell would go a little bit crazy every time he heard this song, made famous by Patti Page. For a few months during Lowell's formative years, it was by far his favorite song.

IAN

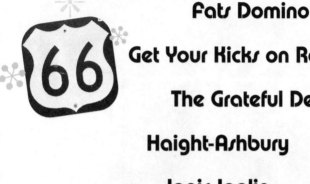

Fats Domino

Get Your Kicks on Route 66

The Grateful Dead

Haight-Ashbury

Janis Joplin

The Lennon Sisters

Les Paul and Mary Ford

The Limbo

The Monkees

Perry Como

Psychedelic music

Purple People Eater

Who would ever remember that Sheb Wooley, who sang this song, was also a character actor in Westerns such as *High Noon*.

The Rolling Stones

Formed in 1962, the Rolling Stones became one of the most famous and enduring rock groups ever. Mick Jagger and Keith Richards first crossed paths at

Dartford Maypole County Primary School and—much later—met up with Brian Jones and Tony Chapman to form the band, which they named after a Muddy Waters song.

The Rolling Stones played their first show on July 12, 1962, at the Marquee. In January of 1963, after a series of personnel changes, Bill Wyman and Charlie Watts rounded out the Stones' line-up. The group soon attracted the attention of manager Andrew Loog Oldham, and in June of 1963, they released their first single, "Come On" (a Chuck Berry tune) and performed on the British TV show *Thank Your Lucky Stars*, where the producer told Oldham to get rid of that "vile-looking singer with the tire-tread lips."

In 1965, the band recorded "(I Can't Get No) Satisfaction," which held the Number 1 spot on the U.S. charts for four weeks and went on to become one of their most popular songs.

Sing Along with Mitch

"Follow the bouncing ball . . ."

The Stroll

The Stroll dance craze was perpetuated by Cookie and the Cupcakes' biggest hit, "Mathilda," which went to Number 1 in south Louisiana and hit Number 47 on the Billboard charts in March 1959. It was a dance we could do solo on the dance floor.

The Watusi

Woodstock

Al Capp

Archie and Veronica

Batman

Bringing Up Father

Dick Tracy

I couldn't wait to read the Sunday funnies so I could join Dick in solving his latest crime caper. But I never could figure out who Bonnie Braids was. Was she his baby? Who was his wife?

Gasoline Alley

Heckle and Jeckle

Jiggs and Maggie

Li'l Abner

Little Iodine

Little Lulu & Tubby

Little Orphan Annie

This popular comic strip was created by Harold Gray in 1924 for the *Chicago Tribune*. Gray's original concept starred a boy named, Otto. Yup, Little Orphan Otto. However, there were many strips featuring boys and none with girls, so Gray changed his character's gender and name.

Little Orphan Annie met do-gooders, crooked politicians, and gangsters, and she fought the Nazis. The strip also had elements of the supernatural. There were ghosts, leprechauns, and Mr. Am, who had lived for "millions of years."

After the success of the Broadway play, Leonard Starr, the artist and writer of *On Stage*, revived the *Little Orphan Annie* comic strip under the title, *Annie*.

Magilla Gorilla

The Many Loves of Dobie Gillis

Mary Worth

Mr. Magoo

Red Ryder and
Little Beaver

Superman

They'll Do It Every Time

Tom Terrific

Winnie Winkle

Babysitting for twenty-five cents per hour

I not only babysat, but I also did the dishes and made sure the house was spic and span after bathing the children and putting them to bed.

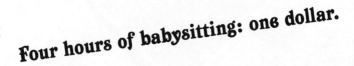

Four hours of babysitting: one dollar.

Bike racks without locks

Bikes with no gears

Cloth diapers

Cotton cloth diapers needed to be rinsed and soaked in a diaper pail with one cup of bleach in the water! It's a wonder our little ones survived.

Clothes hanging on the line

Nothing smells or feels better than a bed made with fresh sheets that have dried on a clothesline in the sunshine and warm breezes. I even remember frozen clothes that stood straight up from drying outside in the winter.

First-class stamps for three cents

Full-service gas stations

Windows washed, oil checked, tires filled—all for *free*!

Hand-cranked water pumps

Letters

Good old-fashioned letters that come in the mail are the best gift you can ever receive because you can read them over and over. And they're so much more personal than today's emails. I miss looking forward to finding letters in my mailbox. However, my mother, bless her heart, continues to write letters to all members of her family.

Thank you, Mom!

Manual reel lawnmowers

Milkmen

Nine-cent movies

Non-air-conditioned cars, homes, and offices

One-room country schools

We ate paste by the jarful. Man, that was good stuff! And I remember recess and our playground: we had swings, teeter-totters, and a merry-go-round that would *never* pass OSHA standards in this day and age. But I don't recall anyone ever getting hurt. When recess was over, the teacher stood on the school porch and rang a hand bell.

Paying with cash

Personally knowing your banker

Root beer stands with waitresses on roller skates

Rural town halls

Dad was on the Long Lake Township Board, and he went to meetings held in a little white town hall building.

Safely leaving cars and houses unlocked

School milk for a dime

Simpler Christmases

Each year we received only *one* present from Santa, and I can still remember most of those gifts. One of the best Christmases ever was the year I received twin baby dolls—*two* dolls—nestled in a blue metal doll bed complete with pillows, sheets, and a blanket that I'm sure now were made by Mom.

We put on Christmas plays in school on a homemade wooden stage with curtains made out of bed sheets dyed black, and kids of all ages took part in Christmas programs at church. The best part of these events was the brown paper bag they handed out to each child. It was filled with ribbon candy, salted-in-the-shell peanuts, and a chocolate drop candy, which I always saved for my dad.

Stores closed on Sunday

Two longs and a short

Back in the days when we didn't have even rotary dial telephones, we had party lines. Each of us on the party line had a special ring that signaled the call was for us. Our special signal during the 1950s was two long rings followed by one short ring.

Walking to school

Wedding receptions in church basements

Fads in Fashion

A-line skirts

Beehive hairdos

Blue jeans, rolled up

Bobby pins

Bobby sox

Bouffant hairstyles

Box-pleated skirts

Brush rollers

Bucket purses

Cardigan sweaters

Cat's-eye glasses

I made Mom take me to the eye doctor where I feigned slightly poor eyesight in order to get a pair of these!

Charm bracelets

We had charms shaped as birthday cakes, miniature signs saying "best friend," wishbones for good luck, graduation caps for—what else—graduation, personal birthstones, and so on—one for every special event or favorite item in our lives. These trinkets are now making a comeback, and our daughters are collecting our charm bracelets and charms as keepsakes.

Chunky shoes

Coonskin hats

Cotton handkerchiefs

Ducktails

Flattops

Garter belts with long, white cotton socks

Ugh! Does anyone else remember these? I was very small when I wore them, but I remember the garter belt went around my chest somehow and was *cold!*

Go-go boots

Granny dresses

Granny glasses

Knee highs

Leisure suits

Men wearing hats

Mini skirts

Mohair sweaters

Narrow ties

Nehru jackets

Organdy aprons

These were worn by friends who were waitresses, coffee pourers, or cake cutters at your wedding.

Paper dresses

Peasant skirts

Pedal pushers

Pillbox hats

Pink foam curlers

Pixie haircuts

Polyester

Poodle Skirts

Pop-bead necklaces

Saddle shoes

School clothes

Dresses and skirts only—we weren't allowed to wear slacks or jeans unless we wore them under our skirts on a freezing cold day.

Spit curls

Starched can cans

String bikinis

Teased hair

White bucks

Wide ties

Women wearing hats

Babes in Toyland

American Flyer trains

Barbie dolls

Baseball cards

Checkers

Chinese Checkers

Easy Bake Oven

G.I. Joe

Homemade dollhouses

Hopalong Cassidy
cap pistols

Hula hoops

Kick the Can

Lionel trains

Marbles

Musical Chairs

Post Office

The kissing game.

Red Rover, Red Rover . . .

Spin the Bottle

Toy surprises

Breakfast cereals during the 1950s contained a vast variety of prizes, such as the little gray plastic submarine—complete with its own "nuclear" fuel—offered by Kellogg's. The fuel turned out to be baking soda, which would cause the submarine to tilt onto its side and "burp," sending it plunging deep into water in your sink or bathtub. At the bottom, it would burp again and rise to the top—over and over.

Cool Stuff

3-D comic books

3-D movies

Autograph books

We had *everyone* sign our autograph books and at slumber parties, we sometimes had autograph dogs (stuffed animals made out of easy-to-write-on fabric).

Black-and-white television

I well remember our first black-and-white television. I also remember that we actually had to get up out of our chairs to turn it on and to change the channels.

Brownie cameras

Brylcreem

Burma-Shave signs

Our love affair with Burma-Shave signs began during the
1950s when mother and father would take us on long
Sunday drives to visit aunts, uncles, and cousins. Just as
we started to get bored in the car, a sequence of Burma-
Shave signs would appear and the trip would immediately
be fun again.

Burma-Shave signs date from the late 1920s. They first
made their appearance in southern Minnesota where we
grew up on a farm. During the Burma-Shave craze, some
7,000 sets popped up all across the United States and
Canada.

Cameras with big, round,
blue flashbulbs

Cinerama movies

Clothespins

Cream separators

Decoder rings

Doilies

Drive-in movies

Edsels

Floral feedsacks used as fabric

I remember having pajamas made out of cotton feed-sacks with a tiny blue-floral print.

Flour sacks made into dish towels

Ford's first Mustangs and Thunderbirds

Frosted root beer mugs

Gillette Blue Blades

Hammocks

Homemade dresses

Horsehair couches

Itchy, itchy, itchy!

Ipana toothpaste

The John Deere Model A

Oilcloth tablecloths

Pepsodent

"You'll wonder where the yellow went when you brush your teeth with Pepsodent."

Record players

Red Ryder air rifles

Silly Putty

**Skeleton keys that
unlocked *any* door**

Slide rules

Studebakers

Timex watches

Toboggans

Vick's Vaporub

After Mom applied this, she'd wrap a flannel scarf lovingly around our necks.

Victrolas

Wax lips

Wooden sleds

Wooden tennis racquets

Aunt Sally molasses
cookies with frosting

Black Jack gum

Black licorice candy pipes

"Breakfast cereal shot from guns"

Bubble Up soda

Candy buttons, candy cigarettes,
and candy lipstick

Cherry Coke

Chocolate Coke

Clove gum

Double Bubble

Dr. Pepper

Dreamsicles

Eskimo Pies

Fizzies

Forever Yours

The Mars Candy Company's dark-chocolate twin to the Milky Way.

Fudgesicles

Hollywood candy bars

These were only five cents each.

Homemade ice cream

Hot dog bubble gum

Krumbles

This breakfast cereal, which you can no longer find because Kellogg's stopped making it, was my grandfather's favorite. So, of course, it was my favorite, too.

Lime phosphates

Nickel Cokes

Nickel ice cream cones

Ovaltine

Penny candy

Popsicles

Sour cream on bread

Our dad showed us this delight. He would take a slice of bread and slather it with sour cream. Then he would sprinkle brown sugar or pour pure maple syrup on top of the sour cream. It was a sweet, farm treat.

Tootsie Rolls

TV dinners

Back-seat bingo

Burn rubber

Daddy-O

Dig it.

Don't get bent out of shape.

Don't have a cow.

Dreamsville

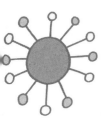

Far out!

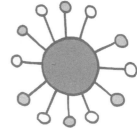

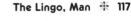

Greaser

I Like Ike.

Lay some skin on me.

Let Hertz put you
in the driver's seat.

Like wow

Pop the clutch.

What's your bag, man?

Wiggin' out

You're cruisin' for a bruisin'.

People in the News

Adlai Stevenson

Althea Gibson

Babe Zaharias-Didrickson

Cassius Clay

He became the most famous boxer of our era and changed his name to Muhammad Ali.

George Mikan

The most popular basketball player in the 1950s, Big George wore number 99 for the old Minneapolis Lakers.

Gladys Gooding

Question: During the late 1940s and the 1950s, who played for the New York Rangers, the New York Knicks, *and* the Brooklyn Dodgers?

Answer: Gladys Gooding, a "Babe" in her own right, who played the organ and sang the National Anthem for all three teams.

Grandma Moses

Houdini

Jack Ruby

Jackie Robinson

Laika

"Laika, long trip?" the Soviets may have asked. Laika was the first dog powered into space by the Soviet Union.

Lee Harvey Oswald

Martin Luther King

Mickey Mantle and Willie Mays

During the 1950s, the best three center fielders in base-ball all played in New York: Mickey Mantle for the Yankees, Willie Mays for the Giants, and Duke Snider for the Dodgers. Arguments rage even today over who was the greatest of them all—the Commerce Comet (Mantle) or the Say Hey Kid (Mays).

Nikita Kruschev

Robert F. Kennedy • • • • • • •

Rocky Marciano

That's the Way It Was

Air-raid drills

We had to get under our desks at school. Now that I think back, what good would that have done?

Bible Camp

Boys working on their cars

We dated boys who had their own cars and wow! what fancy cars they were—spiffed and buffed in bright '50s reds or turquoises. Most of them had stick shifts and were "raked," which meant the fronts were much lower to the ground than the backs. What was the purpose of that?

Bucking

We often gave our friends rides on the backs of our bikes or on the handlebars. We referred to this as "bucking." Even today, some bikes have "bucking handlebars."

Burning bras

The Cold War

The Cuban Missile Crisis

Draft cards

Drag racing

The Eagle has landed.

Fallout shelters

Flying saucers

Free love

Friday night games

Friday night games were the main event in small-town communities. What fun it was to take a bus to another small town for a football or basketball game.

Future Homemakers of America

Going steady

This meant you had to layer fingernail polish over tape wrapped inside your boyfriend's ring—the smoother and thicker the polish, the better.

Hippies

Listening to stories on the radio

I absolutely *loved* to listen to stories on the radio. I will never forget one of my birthdays as a child when the radio announcer said that the next story was for "Jill Larson on her birthday." The story was *The Little Engine That Could*—my favorite! I could not believe that the man on the radio actually knew it was my birthday!

Marshmallow roasts

May baskets

The National Anthem

"The Star Spangled Banner" was played at midnight when our three TV channels shut down for the night. All that was on the screen was a U.S. flag waving in the breeze.

Party lines

Penicillin shots

Pop Art

President Kennedy's assassination

Where were you when it happened?

Riverside picnics

Saturday matinees

Especially double-feature Westerns
at the Princess Theater.

Saturday night dates

School picnics

Scooping the Loop

Slumber parties

Sock hops

Sputnik

Sugar cubes saturated with
the polio vaccine

Sunday drives

Swimming at the lake
or in mudholes

"Under God" added to our
Pledge of Allegiance

A U.S. flag with forty-eight stars

Wiener roasts over bonfires

See ya later, alligator.

After 'while, crocodile.

Photocredits

About the Authors

Jill Larson Sundberg is a baby boomer and business woman, who runs Access Marketing Systems and sells gift items and books to retailers all over the Upper Midwest. She is the author of *My Red Hat* and *My Red Hattitudes* and she helped make the classic *When I Am an Old Woman I Shall Wear Purple* a bestseller. Jill collaborated on this project with her brother Michael Larson, who also attended Long Lake Lutheran Church and St. James High School, in their pre-boomer days. A longtime newspaper editor, Michael Larson now teaches journalism classes at St. Cloud State University and at Minnesota State University, Mankato. Both live in Minnesota.

To Our Readers

Conari Press, an imprint of Red Wheel/Weiser, publishes books on topics ranging from spirituality, personal growth, and relationships to women's issues, parenting, and social issues. Our mission is to publish quality books that will make a difference in people's lives—how we feel about ourselves and how we relate to one another. We value integrity, compassion, and receptivity, both in the books we publish and in the way we do business.

Our readers are our most important resource, and we value your input, suggestions, and ideas about what you would like to see published. Please feel free to contact us, to request our latest book catalog, or to be added to our mailing list.

Conari Press
An imprint of Red Wheel/Weiser, LLC
P.O. Box 612
York Beach, ME 03910-0612
www.conari.com